Walkir

CARDIG
COAST

A guide to a coastal walk from Cardigan to Borth

Liz Allan

Illustrated by Lynne Denman

Cover photographs by Penny Sharp

KITTIWAKE

Published by:
Kittiwake
3 Glantwymyn Village Workshops, Glantwymyn,
Machynlleth, Montgomeryshire SY20 8LY

First edition 2000. Revised edition 2006. Reprint 2007.
Text: © Liz Allan 2006
Illustrations: © Lynne Denman 2006
Cover photographs: © Penny Sharp 2006

Produced on a Macintosh using Photoshop, Freehand and InDesign.

Printed by MWL, Pontypool.

A catalogue record for this book may be found at the British Library.

ISBN: 978 1 902302 38 6

INTRODUCTION

This book was inspired by the many weekends spent exploring the delights of the long distance coastal path in my neighbouring Pembrokeshire. As I visited that splendid county I mused that if I could walk the length of the Pembrokeshire coast, why could I not do the same in my home county of Ceredigion, with its equally spectacular coastline?

Well, for a start, at the time of writing, there is no continuous public right of way along the whole of the coastline. Undeterred by this minor detail, and armed with my local knowledge of quiet country lanes and other foot-paths close to the coast, I set about the happy task of finding a continuous, legal route that linked the coastal town of Cardigan in the south with the coastal town of Borth, some 97 km away in the north. I am happy to say that since first publication of this book in 2000, there have been two new continuous sections of coast path opened; Aberarth to Llanon and Llanrhystud to Aberystwyth. And there's more good news to come as Ceredigion's Coast Path project to create a continuous coast path route from Cardigan to Borth is currently under-way and due to be completed in 2007.

The route is an adventure. A challenge in parts, and easy as pie in others. It has been divided up into six sections – each representing a day's walking which ends in a village or town with accommodation and refreshments. Each of these settlements is served by a regular bus service, (*but check times, particularly if walking in the winter*), so the walk can also be done in individual sections. I do hope, though, that you will be able to find a week of your holidays to discover the whole of this relatively unexplored part of the Welsh coastline. With its internationally important marine wildlife, stunning landscapes, picturesque villages and warm welcomes, I'm sure you will not be disappointed.

During the summers of 2004 and 2005, the *Cardi Bach*, a bus service particularly aimed for walkers, operated from New Quay to Cardigan visiting the many coastal villages and towns en route. It is hoped to continue to operate *Cardi Bach* in future years.

About the author:
Liz Allan was born in South Wales where she spent most of her child-
hood exploring the Gower coast through play. Having lived and worked in
Australia and London, she now lives in New Quay in Ceredigion. She has
worked for Ceredigion County Council since 1992 and is their Conservation
Management Officer. She has a MSc in Protected Landscape Management
from the University of Wales, Aberystwyth and believes strongly in both the
conservation and enjoyment of our natural environment.

About the illustrator:
Lynne Denman was born and raised near the sea in Somerset and later Jersey.
She learned to love the mountains as well when her family moved to the
North of England. She married a Welshman and found all her favourite landscapes together in West Wales, along with an ancient language and lively
culture thrown into the bargain. She is a practising artist and exhibition
designer, working mostly in the field of local and natural history.

Photography by:
Penny Sharp, originally from Yorkshire, but now a local photographer who
specialises in land and seascapes.

Contents

Cardigan to Aberporth

11 miles/18 kilometres

Cardigan to Mwnt

6 miles/10 kilometres

Cardigan – the gateway to Ceredigion – The ancient borough of Cardigan received its first charter in 1199 and was once considered to be the second most important port in Wales. Shipbuilding flourished during the 19th century and was centred around the Netpool area where this walk begins.

Just west of Cardigan Bridge, the Netpool recreation ground is found at the far end of the car-park at Somerfield supermarket. Take the path from the car-park near the floating restaurant up the bank to the pagoda in the recreation ground. Follow the lane past the Hyder Cardigan Waste Water Treatment sign along the bank of the river. The path is sign-posted at the Sewage Treatment works (that's the bad bit!), but there are good views of the Afon Teifi where you can watch for a variety of wading birds, including redshank and curlew.

At 'Old Castle Farm', turn right onto the farm lane and continue uphill until you reach a T- junction where you turn left. Follow this quiet lane until you arrive at the entrance to Rhos Fach farm, and a footpath sign on the right. Go through the kissing gate (marked no. 12) and keep to the left hand side of the fields. The path emerges onto the road to Gwbert.

Cross over and turn right and, after 10 metres, you will reach a bridle gate on the left. The path now passes in front of a house, crosses a bridge, through another bridle gate and passes to the right of a second house before reaching an old track which leads into some woods.

Where the path emerges from the woods, turn left and follow the track until you reach the farm 'Bryn Pedwr'. Turn right at the footpath sign and continue straight ahead past a new farm building on your left to a field gate across the field. The path continues to a permissive access area with a bench and the remains of a mud wall cottage. Over the stile the path continues alongside the stream until a stile in the right hand corner of the field. Turning right you reach the small hamlet of Y Ferwig. Turn left onto the road and follow the road uphill past an old AA sign, telling you that you are 235½ miles from London, until you reach the farm lane straight ahead of you with a 'No Through Road' sign. This lane passes by several farm buildings and a duck pond. Cross the cattle grid leading to 'Nantycroi Farm' (B&B and camping/touring facilities) and enter the farm yard. A faded green man sign points to the left to a track leading to Mwnt.

Follow this track and enjoy the coastal views of Cardigan Island, which is now a nature reserve managed by the local Wildlife Trust. Puffins used to nest there, but rats wiped them out when they got onto the island from a ship that had been wrecked on the rocks. Efforts by the Wildlife Trust to re-introduce puffins to the island have, to date, proved unsuccessful. About 4000 pairs of lesser black-backed gulls now nest there. Where the track ends at a field gate, turn left and follow the fence-bank to the kissing gate. Turn right onto the coastal path which leads you directly down into Mwnt. Some of the best displays of Spring Squill can be found on the long-abandoned arable fields along the cliff tops to the east.

The sheltered sandy cove, ideal for swimming, is a National Trust property. From the vantage point of the conical outcrop known as Foel y Mwnt, bottlenose dolphins, harbour porpoise and, more rarely, basking shark and sunfish can sometimes be seen close into shore. It's also an excellent spot to watch for choughs.

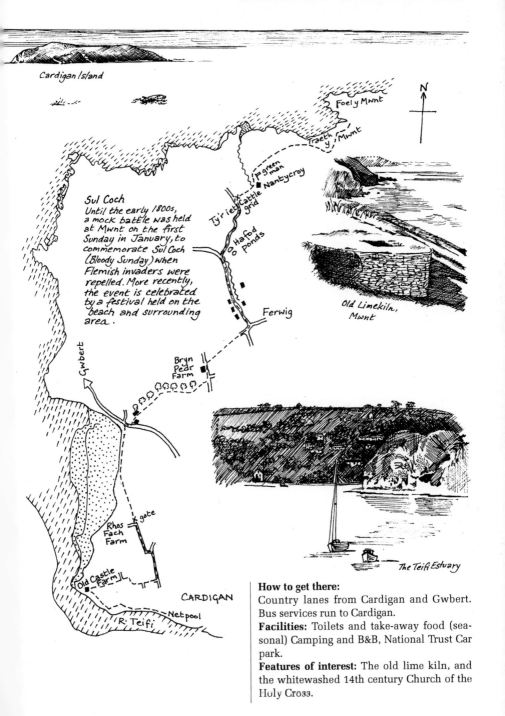

Cardigan Island

Foel y Mwnt

N

Traeth y Mwnt

green man

Nantycroy

Sul Coch

Until the early 1800s, a mock battle was held at Mwnt on the first Sunday in January, to commemorate Sul Coch (Bloody Sunday) when Flemish invaders were repelled. More recently, the event is celebrated by a festival held on the beach and surrounding area.

Tyriet

cattle grid

Hafod ponds

Ferwig

Old Limekiln, Mwnt

Gwbert

Bryn Pedr Farm

Rhos Fach Farm

gate

Old Castle Farm

CARDIGAN

Netpool

R. Teifi

The Teifi Estuary

How to get there:
Country lanes from Cardigan and Gwbert. Bus services run to Cardigan.
Facilities: Toilets and take-away food (seasonal) Camping and B&B, National Trust Car park.
Features of interest: The old lime kiln, and the whitewashed 14th century Church of the Holy Cross.

Mwnt to Aberporth
5 miles/8 kilometres

There is no coastal path from Mwnt to Aberporth, so the route follows a country lane, and public footpaths over fields.

Leave Mwnt by following the lane which runs between the car-park and the church. Continue along the lane through a gate to 'Ty Gwyn Caravan and Camping'. The lane crosses over a stream and becomes a track. Pass the bungalow 'Min-y-mor' and 'Ty Gwyn Farm' on your right and then continue up the hill through a field gate to another field gate that is the start of an old track (soggy in places). At the top of this track continue straight ahead and pass in front of a farm building towards a pair of metal gates. The gates lead into a small caravan site. Continue along a concrete track uphill, cross the cattle-grid and turn left along the road. This next stretch of the walk is along a metalled road which, after 100 metres, bears right, but follow the lane which goes straight on. This lane carries on for half a mile or so.

At the point where the lane bears right, and the entrance to 'Pen-y-graig Farm' is on

8

your left, look straight ahead in amongst a hedge-bank to spot a stile set back from the lane just beyond a small spring. The route is now about to take you across fields and farms for the next 45 minutes or so of walking, before reaching the entrance to the Qinetiq range at Aberporth, which provides a controlled environment for the release of land, sea and air launched missile firings.

So, cross two stiles that lead into the right hand field and continue across the field until the derelict farm of 'Mwnt mawr' is reached. Cross the stile and follow the direction of the way-mark to pass the old farm on

your left. The path continues across the field towards the property 'Mwnt bach'. The path has recently been diverted here and there is a sign pointing to the line of the diverted route about 20 metres away and set back into the hedge-bank.

The path crosses a two-sleeper bridge and turns right over the stile onto a track that leads to the farm 'Ffrwdwenith - isaf' Turn right over the stile and pass the farm along the track to a finger-post on your left. Follow the path that runs along the left hand side of the field to a stile and kissing gate. Through the gate keep to the right-hand side of the field and continue straight ahead towards a gap into the next field until you reach a kissing gate leading out onto a lane. Turn left and at the farm, 'Ffrwdwenith-uchaf' look for the permissive path sign-post on your right, about 50 metres from the farm entrance. Cross the stile and go left, passing over three more stiles to a farm track where you turn right. At the end of this short track, cross over the stile straight ahead over you and continue along the right edge of the field to a field-gate and overgrown stile. Carry on straight ahead past a field gate on right to a small two sleeper bridge and kissing gate.

Go through a gate, turn left to stile into a wooded scrub area. The track continues down the slope to a small bridge on your right and another stile. Cross here and the path continues diagonally right to a white post amongst an old hedge bank visible on the sky-line. The path continues diagonally right over the field to a kissing gate and onto another kissing gate next to the entrance to the Qinetiq establishment. Turn right. At the T-junction, turn left past the football pitches. After 100 metres or so, turn left at the road with a bus shelter and toilet block on its corner. This road now takes you directly down to the two beaches at Aberporth..

How to get there:
B4333 from Blaenannerch or the Gogerddan Arms public house. Car parking. Regular daily bus services between Cardigan and Aberaeron

Facilities: Shops (PO), cafes and pubs. Public toilets. Accommodation

Aberporth to Llangrannog
5½ miles/8½ kilometres

Aberporth to Tresaith
1½ miles/2 kilometres

Easy, straightforward walking along the cliffs

This cliff top walk starts from the footpath leading up from the north beach, Traeth Dyffryn. Follow the road for a few metres until you see a footpath sign on the left. Continue along the small lane and cross a small car-park to the start of the cliff walk. The coast path passes some curious converted old railway carriages, now used as holiday accommodation. As you begin your descent down the steps into the resort of Tresaith, the waterfall of the Afon Saith cascading onto the beach can be clearly seen.

How to get there: Two miles from A487 at the Tanygroes Car Dismantlers. Bus services between Aberporth and Tresaith from Cardigan and Synod Inn.
Facilities: Public toilets. Beach take-away. Inn. Hostel. Limited car parking spaces at beach. Good access for people with disabilities along an upgraded section from the small car-park at Aberporth out onto the cliff path

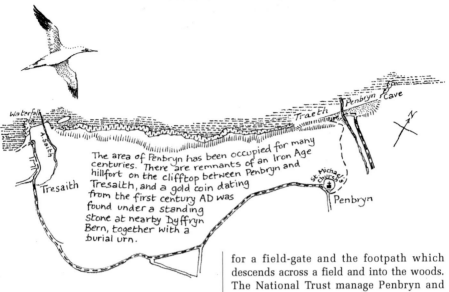

The area of Penbryn has been occupied for many centuries. There are remnants of an Iron Age hillfort on the clifftop between Penbryn and Tresaith, and a gold coin dating from the first century AD was found under a standing stone at nearby Dyffryn Bern, together with a burial urn.

Tresaith to Penbryn
2 miles/3½ kilometres

There is no coast path between Tresaith and Penbryn, so this next stretch is entirely along quiet country lanes. A through coastpath route to Penbryn is scheduled to be completed by 2007.

Climb the hill road to leave Tresaith, and at the top turn left. The road continues to climb uphill. Where the road flattens out, take the first turning on the left and continue along this small lane until you reach a T-junction.

Turn left, and the road now descends into Penbryn, passing a farm which makes organic cheese. Continuing downhill, St. Michael's Church, said to be one of the oldest churches in Wales, comes into view and is well worth a visit.

Beyond the church on the left look out for a field-gate and the footpath which descends across a field and into the woods. The National Trust manage Penbryn and have created a path through these woods from the church to the beach. The beach, Traeth Penbryn, is three quarters of a mile in length, and can be reached from Tresaith with care at low tide. But be careful as the cliffs crumble easily, and on no account should they be climbed.

The path from the beach follows the access road until it reaches a farm, small car park and café.

How to get there:
1¾ miles from A487 at Sarnau.
Facilities: Café (seasonal). Public toilets (seasonal). National Trust car parking.

Penbryn

Penbryn to Llangrannog
2 miles/3 kilometres

This lovely walk to the small seaside village of Llangrannog follows the coastal path all the way.

From the Llanborth car park at Penbryn, the footpath is sign-posted at the left of the farm. Through field-gates, an ancient track-way climbs the gorse, heather and bracken covered hill and gives fine views of the sweep of Penbryn beach and the coast beyond.

A stile on the left at the top of the climb leads away from the track, and the path now crosses fields and descends to pass close to a small sandy cove, before climbing steeply once more to the cliff tops. This path is well sign-posted and easily followed all the way to the pretty little village of Llangrannog.

A notable landmark on the beach at Llangrannog is the rocky stack known as Devil's Tooth or Carreg Bica. The story goes that one day the Devil had a raging toothache, and in desperation to rid himself of the pain, plucked the offending fang from his mouth and hurled it into the air, whereupon it fell to Earth and landed on Llangrannog

beach, where it remains to this day. Another interesting legend of this small village surrounds the Celtic saint, St. Carantoc, and how he came to found Llangrannog sometime around 500 AD. The legend says that when St. Carantoc was making a new staff in his cave in the hills, a pigeon swooped down and carried away a piece of bark from it. The saint decided that this could be a message from God and so followed the pigeon to see where it would take the bark. The pigeon flew into the Llangrannog valley and laid the bark near the site of the present church. The Celtic Saint believed that this must be God's chosen place, and so built the first church with wattle and daub. St. Carnog's church was rebuilt in 1884 and can be found a short walk up the hill from the beach.

How to get there:
B4321 from A487 at Brynhoffnant (2 miles); B4334 from Pentregat (3½ miles). Bus service **Facilities:** Car-parking. Beach cafés. Pubs. Shop. Public toilets. Accommodation.

*Carreg Bicca
Llangranog*

Llangranog is the birthplace of the County's most celebrated teacher of navigation - one 'Cranogwen', Sarah Jane Rees. Born in 1838 she acquired her master mariner's certificate and taught in the village school. She coached generations of local boys in the art of deep-sea navigation and died in 1916.

Llangrannog to New Quay
9 miles/14½ kilometres

Llangranog to Cwmtudu
5 miles/8½ kilometres

The coastal path continues north for a short distance only, but passes some of the most spectacular scenery in Ceredigion. The route then comes a little inland along a lovely wooded valley to the small hamlet of Cwmtudu. Alternatively at the B432, take the route along lovely quiet country lanes to Cwmtudu that is now also a Cycle Route.

Take the steps leaving the northern end of the beach, past the Patio Café. The coastal path climbs towards Pen y Badell, an imposing Celtic Hill Fort. When you reach the gate directly in front of you, turn left along the track and circumnavigate the Hill Fort which is covered in purple heather and yellow gorse during summer. Listen for the sounds of chough, a blackbird-like bird with red legs and beak, or the screech of the peregrine overhead. Looking down at the promontory, the small island of Ynys Lochtyn lies beneath you. This is a good place to watch for harbour porpoise and bottlenose dolphins feeding, or grey seals popping their heads above the waves.

The path continues around the side of the hill,

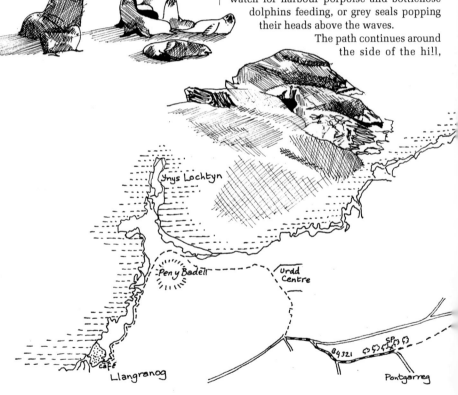

before rising steeply and continuing north to follow the cliff top to the Urdd Centre with its' dry ski slope. This is one of two Urdd Gobaith Cymru centres (Welsh Youth Movement) that offers over 15,000 youngsters a variety of activities throughout the year. Leave the coast now, and descend towards the Centre, where the route continues down along the Urdd access road until it reaches a cross-road with the B4321.

Turn left and follow this road bearing right in the direction of Pontgarreg. The road passes a wood on the left, and at the end of this small wood, just as you reach the small hamlet of Pontgarreg, a bench on the left guides you along the edge of these woodlands towards a stile and across some fields. The path then emerges onto a quiet country lane past the property 'Frondeg'. Turn right along the lane and continue until you reach a left-hand turn, sign-posted Cwmtudu. Go left here and follow the road for about 400 metres, looking for a stile set back from the road on the right. Climb the stile and follow the path along this secluded valley until it passes some properties and emerges onto the road. Turn right and then left at the staggered crossroads. Follow this road which continues to wind its way along the lovely wooded valley of Afon Ffynnon-Ddewi until you reach the small hamlet of Cwmtudu.

If you want to try the cycle route alternative, turn left onto the B4321 and where the road bears right in the direction of Pontgarreg, go straight ahead to follow the Gilfach Caravan Park sign. Continue uphill to where road curves to right and a signpost to Cwmtudu. Take this single track road straight ahead and continue until a signpost points you to the left. The road now descends through lovely woodland to the staggered crossroads, where you turn left onto the road into Cwmtudu.

How to get there:
Country lanes from A487 to Llwyndafydd.
Facilities: Public toilets. Car parking. Take-away and café (seasonal). Camping.
Features of interest: Restored lime kiln

Birds Rock

Castell Bach

Pen-y-graig

Cwmtudu gate

Afon Su

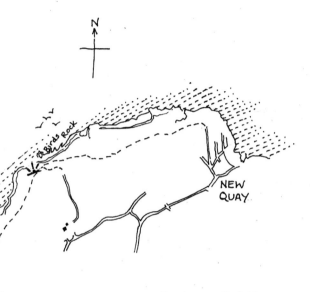

NEW
QUAY

Cardigan Bay Bottlenose Dolphins
The population in the Bay of these
fascinating marine mammals is estimated
to be around 130 animals. Bottlenose dolphins
can grow up to 4m. in length and live for
30 years or more. Adult females have one
calf every two to three years during March
to September and these young take 18months
or so to wean. If you spot two dorsal fins
very close together, take a close look, as
these are likely to be a mother with her calf.

Well defined coast-path all the way passing by secluded coves and wooded valleys.

The small cove of Cwmtudu is owned by the National Trust. The old lime kiln that is set back from the beach has been recently restored, and in their heyday they were used to burn limestone brought in by boat from Pembrokeshire. Farmers from the surrounding countryside would come by horse and cart to collect the lime for spreading on their fields as a fertiliser. This small cove and surrounding caves were also once used by smugglers bringing in goods such as French brandy and salt. The contraband was hidden in dark, secluded caves until it could safely be carried inland on horseback.

The rocks and caves just south of Cwmtudu are known locally as Seals Bay. There are estimated to be just over 4700 grey seals in the West Wales area and along this stretch of coastline approximately 17 seal pups are born every year between September to December The grey seal can spend up to 80% of the time submerged when they are at sea looking for food, and they can stay underwater during a short dive for up to 8 minutes. They use Seals Bay to haul out onto the rocks to rest in between their feeding excursions.

From Cwmtudu, the coast-path leaves the cove from the kissing gate at the northern end of the beach. The gradual climb up gorse and bracken covered slopes brings you to a fine viewing point. Looking ahead, the remains of small earthen banks of the Iron Age promontory fort, Castell Bach. which was occupied from around the 3rd century BC for about 400 years by a small tribe of Celts, can be seen. The path continues to Pen y graig farm and along a track, then descends through a field on the left to the delightful wooded valley of Cwm Soden and Byrlip.

Wood anemone, wild primrose, wood sorrel, bluebells and early purple orchids abound in the Spring and early summer alongside the Afon Soden with it's cascading mini-waterfall. Cross over the bridges and follow the path to the left as it continues north out towards a lovely sheltered cove. The coast-path continues along the cliffs, descending at one point to pass through the sheltered area of Coybal, with its steep slopes covered in blackthorn.

When you reach the old white walled coast-guard hut, now restored to the Cardigan Bay Lookout, keep an eye open for the most important seabird breeding colony in Ceredigion – Craig yr Adar (Birds Rock). Pass the lookout hut. The path descends for a few metres until you reach a small quarried area. Spend a few moments here looking over the cliff, and from spring to early summer you will be rewarded with the sight of nearly 3000 guillemots crammed onto the bare rock ledges. Razorbills, kittiwakes, fulmar, cormorants, shags and lesser black-backed gulls also breed here. This is also a good area to watch for seals. Continue along the well defined coast path through an interesting area of submaritime heath on uncultivated sea-cliff slopes at the headland above New Quay. The path emerges at Lewis Terrace, one of three fine terraces which overlook Cardigan Bay and give marvellous views (on a clear day) towards the Llyn Peninsula. Continue until you see a finger-post on the left to a path leading behind some houses. This path emerges onto the middle terrace, Marine Terrace, where you continue down towards the harbour.

How to get there:
A486 from A487 at Synod Inn. B4324 from Llanarth. Buses from Aberystwyth and Cardigan.
Facilities: Car parking. Public toilets. Pubs. Cafes. Shops. PO. Bank. Accommodation. Tourist Information Centre (seasonal).
Features of interest: Wildlife boat trips. Harbour. Heritage Centre. Cardigan Bay Marine Wildlife Centre.

New Quay to Llanrhystud
16 miles/25 kilometres

As well as some fine cliff-top walking, much of this section of the walk is along the beach and provides many an opportunity to study first hand the old cliff-line along the coast prior to the last Ice Age. The sediments deposited during that time and since are spectacularly displayed between New Quay and Cei Bach, and between Aberaeron and Aberarth.

New Quay to Aberaeron
6 miles/9 kilometres

Setting off on this next stretch of coastal path MUST coincide with low water, as this is the only possible way to walk along the beach Traeth Gwyn to Llanina Point. *Check the times of the tides at the Harbourmaster's hut on the Quay.* Otherwise, you will have to walk along the B4324 that leads to Llanarth, turning left just beyond Quay West Caravan Park at the signpost to Cei Bach. If you take this route you will be following in famous footsteps, as it was along this lane that Dylan Thomas used to walk during his trips from his home at the bungalow, 'Majoda' to the various hostelries in New Quay – notably the Black Lion.

Ina, the 7th century King of the West Saxons famous as the builder of Glastonbury Abbey, was supposedly shipwrecked at Llanina Point but was rescued by some local people. To show his gratitude, he built a church which is now said to be lost beneath the waves, but whose eerie bell can sometimes be still heard on dark, stormy nights. The present church just visible from the beach, was built in 1850. At Llanina Point the stream is passable only during a dry spell, allowing you to carry on along the beach to Cei Bach where you leave the beach via the access track. Continue past the caravan park, car-park and pub to the T-junction. Continue straight ahead and turn left along the path that leads to the property 'Llwynon'.

If, however, you head for Cei Bach via the road, turn right at the T-junction that points left towards Ceit Bach and the path is a few metres up on your left. The coastal path north to Aberaeron starts again here. Look to your left as you approach the prop-

erty 'Llwynon' and follow the path leading into the copse. The path gently climbs again through wooded areas and open fields, up onto the open of the bracken covered slopes. Resist the temptation to follow any paths that lead away to the right. The path passes over a waterfall where the Afon Drwyi cascades into the sea and climbs again across the gorse-covered slope. The line of the coastal path would benefit from some sign-posting at this point as it has become quite confusing as the result of recently formed tracks from the nearby quad biking establishment and, one suspects, from people trying to make their way up the slope the best they can. Once at the top the path continues across bracken slopes, then farmland and finally along a track (wonderful for blackberry picking) to the holiday village at Gilfach yr Halen, which was formerly a dairy farm.

Pass through the yard alongside the building on your left and turn left down along the road. Keep following this road for about 500 metres until you see the signs on your left directing you across some fields back onto the coast-path. The coastal path now continues all the way to the Georgian harbour town of Aberaeron.

How to get there:
A487 and A482. Bus service from Cardigan, Aberystwyth, Lampeter, Carmarthen.
Facilities: Car parking. Public toilets. Pubs. Cafés. Shops. PO. Banks. Acccommodation. Tourist Information Centre.
Features of interest: Wildlife boat trips. Local crafts centre. Vineyard.

New Quay Head

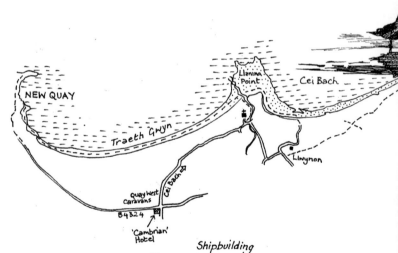

Shipbuilding

The great era of maritime history in the County peaked during the 19th century. New Quay was the most important shipbuilding centre with some 240 vessels being built at New Quay and Cei Bach between 1800-1882 by at least nine different builders. There are few signs left along the coast of this heyday, save for a few ruined limekilns and harbours that are now full of pleasure craft.

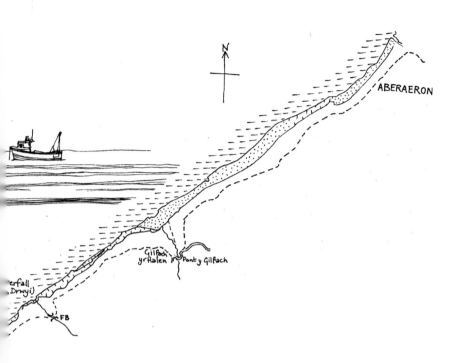

N

ABERAERON

Gilfach
yr Halen · Pont y Gilfach

·erfall
Drwyi)

FB

New Quay

Aberaeron to Llanrhystud
10 miles/16 kilometres

The coastal path from here has now been eroded but access is still possible along the foreshore from the north beach at Aberaeron to the small quiet village of Aberarth, one of the earliest settlements along the Ceredigion coast. On the shore at low tide, clearly visible to the south of the village, are the remains of large semi-circular walls of stone which are thought to date back to the 6th century. These walls are the remains of fish traps, stranding fish such as salmon, sprats and mullet as the tide went out.

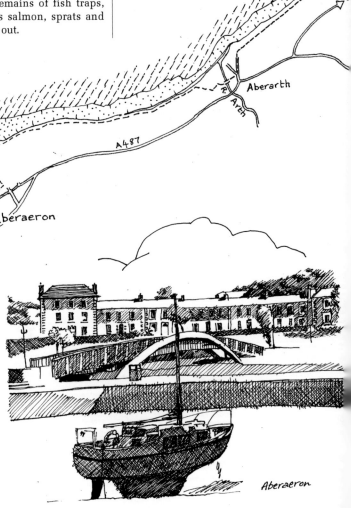

Aberaeron

Dolphins (not sharks!)

Leave the rocky beach Aberarth via the concrete steps and take the first left after a row of cottages. Follow this little village lane as it winds its way down to a bridge crossing the Arth river with its small waterfalls and deep pools. Crossing the bridge, turn left at the lane and take the next lane on the right marked with a 'green man' sign towards the access to the beach. At the end of this lane at the start of the path back to the beach, there is a field-gate on your right that at the time of walking (December 2005) was not yet sign-posted. This is the start of the coast-path to Llanrhystud. Through the field gate, continue up the slope and across the field to a kissing-gate. There has been bad erosion of these soft cliffs and the original line of the path has been lost. As part of the Ceredigion Coast Path project a new path has been created to allow for this section of coast to be opened up again to walkers. Keep going straight ahead to a second kissing gate where an old track on the left leads the way ahead. This is a lovely old track bordered by blackthorn, alongside the cliff-top and makes for very pleasant, gentle walking. Follow the directions of two coastpath posts and continue along the path as it crosses over a small stream cascading down the cliffs. The path then begins its descent toward the sweep of Llanon beach.

The path crosses two stiles and a tiny trickle of a stream (two stepping stones) and continues ahead across the field to a finger-post pointing right by another stream (this one is bigger but with no bridge, but passable). Cross over the stile that has an orange 'Tir Gofal' (Wales agri-environmental scheme) way-mark sign and continue across several open flat fields to where the path emerges at the lane to the beach near Morfa Mawr Hotel and Restaurant.

There are now two options. Either a short walk along the beach, if the tide is favourable, to join a path leading away from the beach to walk along the quiet village lanes in the direction of the church. Or a right turn along the beach access lane to the main A487 road where you turn left and walk along the pavement for about 150 metres into Llanon village. Continue along the main road until you reach a small lane on the left. The church of St. Fraed (St.Bridget) – the patron saint of dairy maids – is clearly visible ahead of you, so head straight for that as the path to Llanrhystud starts at the left of the church

along an old pilgrim road. There is a second church dedicated to another female saint here – St. Non – whose son, St. David, was reputedly born in Llanon around 500 AD.

But back to our old pilgrim road. This gives way to a path which crosses fields after a short while, and continues through kissing gates before coming out at a group of lime kilns. This area is managed by the Wildlife Trust West Wales as an ancient monument site and wildlife nature reserve. The path continues with the kilns on your right until it reaches a stile with an arrow pointing to a footpath on your right.

Llanon

Aberaeron
(A487)

Cross the stile and turn left instead, as your route now must carry on along the terraced storm beach of large pebbles. If you walk along the top 'terrace' of this beach, not only will it save you a climb back up from the beach later, but it will be easier to spot the small car-parking area. It is there that you need to leave the beach and walk along the lane until nearly reaching the main A487 and the Shell garage looming in front of you.

Just before the main road, turn left at the sign to Pencarreg Caravan Park and continue along the lane until reaching the site, which is the start of the next section of your walk.

How to get there:
A487; B4337. Regular buses to Aberystwyth and Aberaeron
Facilities: PO. Shop, pub, garage with restaurant, accommodation, Penrhos Golf and Leisure Club with accommodation a short walk away along the B4337

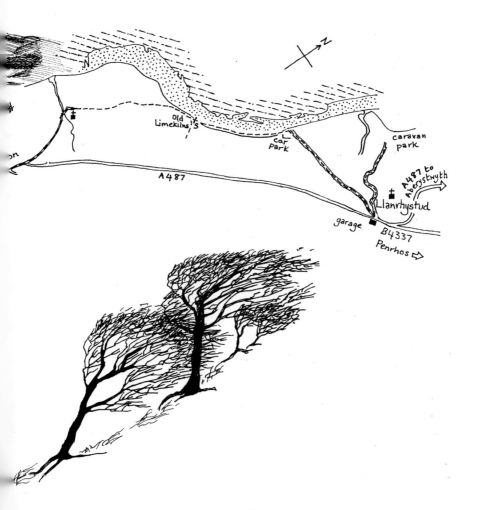

Llanrhystud to Aberystwyth
11 miles/17½ kilometres

This long, wild stretch of coastline is one of the most remote in Ceredigion and gives stunning views of Aberystwyth and Constitution Hill. There is now a continuous coastal path thanks to a recent footpath creation between the National Trust property of Mynachdy'r graig and the derelict farm building 'Ffos-las'.

The sign-posted path starts at the Pencarreg Caravan site and follows the top of the touring caravan field to a stile, then continues across farmland before descending to a small wooden bridge. Crossing the bridge, the path climbs steeply and then winds its way through bracken and gorse covered slopes. In summer this path can get quite overgrown, so take extra care. The peaceful solitude that awaits you is well worth the effort of bashing back the bracken. The Wildlife Trust of South & West Wales reserve at Penderi is interesting; a windblown oak woodland on the steep coastal slope probably of great age. This is also a good spot for watching seals on the rocks below. The path descends through the bracken covered slopes to emerge onto open flat fields. Cross the stile where it emerges and continue straight ahead across the fields with the fence line on your left. This path leads to the white-washed old farm buildings of Mynachdy'r Graig. Follow the coast path sign to the stile beyond the front of the farmhouse, and continue across the fields crossing another four stiles as you head

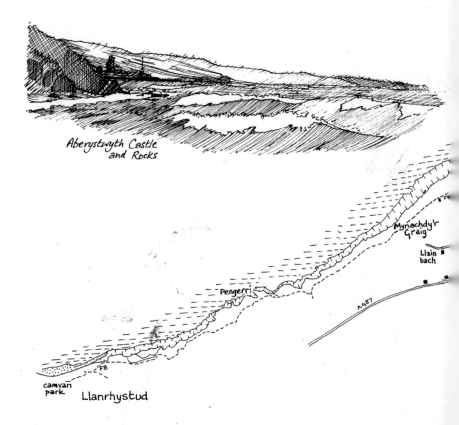

Aberystwyth Castle and Rocks

Mynachdy'r Graig

Llain bach

Pengerri

A487

FB

camvan park

Llanrhystud

north along the cliff-top. At the 6th stile from Mynachdy'r, go straight ahead up the path leading up the slope to another coastpath sign that points left along a track leading down to the derelict Ffos Las. Approaching the old farm buildings, a coast path sign on the right points downwards to a track leading away to the right. This bridle way continues, climbs and passes through an old hawthorn 'arch' to where it meets at a T-junction with another track Turn right and follow this track until it emerges onto the access road to Morfa Bychan Caravan Park.

Turn left and follow the road down until you see a coastal path sign on the right. This final stretch of path into Aberystwyth offers some of the finest views of the whole of Ceredigion. Looking east from the high ridge you will see the Cambrian Mountains with the summit of Plynlimon; to the south New Quay headland and Cardigan Island; and ahead Ceredigion's northern boundary of the Dyfi Estuary.

The path descends steeply to Tanybwlch beach, the best shingle beach in Ceredigion, designated a Site of Special Scientific Interest because of its distinctive plant communities. Look out for the unusual prostrate black-thorn buried deep in the shingle, thought to be probably 200 years old. This area is now part of a Local Nature Reserve, dominated by the imposing Hill Fort of Pen Dinas and Wellington monument. Carry on walking along the beach to the harbour at Aberystwyth, the largest town in the County.

How to get there:
A487; A44; A4120. Bus and train services.
Facilities: PO. Banks. Shops. Cafes and restaurants. Accommodation. Tourist Information Centre.
Features of Interest: Arts Centre, National Library of Wales; Museum, Devils Bridge steam railway

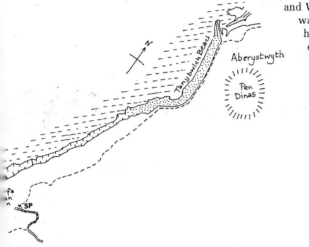

Pen Dinas

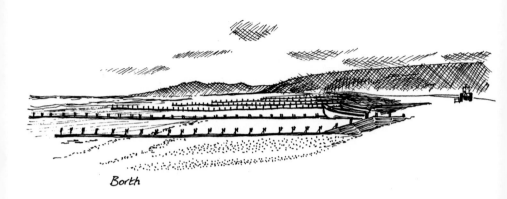

Borth

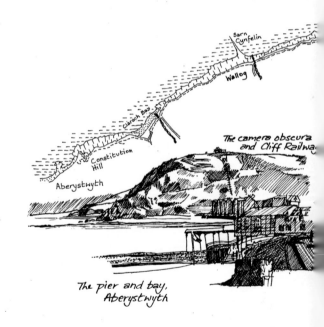

Sarn Cynfelin

Wallog

The camera obscura and Cliff Railway

Clarach Bay

Constitution Hill

Aberystwyth

The pier and bay, Aberystwyth

Dyfi Estuary

Ynyslas

N

Borth

Upper Borth

Dunes at Ynys las

Aberystwyth to Ynyslas
9 miles/15 kilometres

Coastal path all the way to Borth. Very steep stretches from Wallog, but a gentle stroll along the fine sandy beach from Borth to Ynyslas to finish.

Leave the town of Aberystwyth by the footpath leading up to Constitution Hill at the northern end of North Beach. Alternatively during the summer months, take a ride up on the clifftop railway. At the summit, there is a café and the largest Camera Obscura in the world. Follow the coastal path which passes in front of the café and continue along a well trodden path to the beach at Clarach. Clarach is a holiday village of caravans; busy in summer but quiet as the grave in the winter.

To the north of the beach by the Leisure Centre, an ancient track rises up the hill between stone and earth banks. These soft clay cliffs have become quite badly eroded in parts, but this section soon gives way to more stable terrain after Wallog. Extending from the shore at Wallog is the impressive Sarn Cynfelin. A feature unique to Cardigan Bay and part of the Pen Llyn a'r Sarnau Special Area of Conservation, this ridge is 20 yards wide and extends out below the surface of the sea for seven miles. It is thought to be a morrainic feature dating from the last Ice Age. A lime kiln, recently restored, is also of interest at Wallog.

This exhilarating stretch of coastal path continues with some steep sections to the popular seaside resort of Borth. A common site along the way are cormorants perched on the rocks below drying their wings. Cormorants, like other seabirds, need to submerge to feed on a variety of small fish, molluscs and small crustaceans. Cormorants have wider spaced barbs on their feathers than other divers , enabling them to catch prey at much greater depths and so can easily become waterlogged. The snag is that, after surfacing, they have difficulty in taking off and must then perch on a rock with wings outstretched to dry out!

The coastal path ends at the War Memorial, where there is a small car park. There are exceptionally fine views from here to the Dyfi estuary, Ynyslas and the bogland of Cors Fochno, all part of the Dyfi National Nature Reserve. The estuary is one of the most important areas for migrant waders and wildfowl in Cardigan Bay with flocks of wigeon, teal, pintail and the only flock of greenland white-fronted geese regularly occurring in Wales. Years ago it was possible to catch a steam ferryboat across to Aberdyfi from Ynyslas Point, but nowadays you have to go by road or rail to Machynlleth to cross the river.

Beyond, the Snowdonia National Park looms. Either continue along the road through the village, or at low water follow the long sandy beach to the sand-dunes at Ynyslas and journey's end.

How to get there:
B4353 from Rhydypennau or Trerddol. Bus service to Aberystwyth. BR from Aberystwyth to Shrewsbury.

Facilities: Ynyslas Visitor Centre (seasonal). Shops, pubs, PO, accommodation, Car parks at Ynyslas (Dyfi National Nature Reserve); Borth Golf Club.

Features of interest: Stumps of a 6000 year old submerged forest of alder, pine, oak and hazel on Borth/Ynyslas beach

WELSH
The meanings of some of the commom words found in local place names

aber	mouth	**glyder**	heap	**plas**	mansion
afon	river,	**glyn**	glen	**porth**	port
	stream	**gors**	bog	**pwll**	pool
allt	hillside	**grug**	heather		
		gwen	white	**rhaeadr**	waterfall
bach	small	**gyrn**	peak	**rhiw**	hill
banc	hill			**rhos**	marsh,
blaen	head of	**hafod**	summer		moor
	valley	dwelling		**rhyd**	ford
bont	bridge	**hen**	old		
bryn	hill	**hendre**	winter	**sarn**	road
bwlch	pass	dwelling		**sych**	dry
		heol	road		
cadair	chair	**hir**	long	**tarren**	hill
caer	fort			**tomen**	mound
capel	chapel	**isaf**	lowest	**traeth**	shore,
castell	castle				beach
cefn	ridge	**llan**	church	**traws**	across
ceunant	ravine	**llech**	slate	**tref**	hamlet,
coch	red	**llidiart**	gate		home
coed	wood	**llwyd**	grey	**twll**	hole
craig	rock	**llyn**	lake	**ty**	house
croes	cross				
cwm	valley	**maen**	stone	**uchaf**	highest
		maes	field		
dinas	fort, city	**mawr**	big	**y, yr**	the, of the
dol	meadow	**melin**	mill	**ynys**	island
du	black	**moch**	pigs	**ysgol**	school
dwr	water	**moel**	bare hill	**ystrad**	valley
dyffryn	valley	**mor**	sea		floor
		mynach	monk		
eglwys	church	**mynydd**	mountain		
esgair	hillspur				
		nant	stream		
fach	small	**neuadd**	hall		
fan	high place	**newydd**	new		
fawr	large				
fechan	small	**ogof**	cave		
felin	mill				
ffordd	road	**pandy**	mill		
ffynnon	spring, well	**pant**	hollow		
foel	bare hill	**parc**	field, park		
fynydd	mountain	**pen**	top		
garth	enclosure,	**penmaen**	rocky		
hill			headland		
glas	green,	**pistyll**	waterfall,		
blue			spout		

31

PRONUNCIATION

These basic points should help non-Welsh speakers

Welsh	English equivalent
c	always hard, as in cat
ch	as in the Scottish word loch
dd	as th in then
f	as v in vocal
ff	as f
g	always hard as in got
ll	no real equivalent. It is like 'th' in then, but with an 'L' sound added to it, giving 'thlan' for the pronunciation of the Welsh 'Llan'.

In Welsh the accent usually falls on the last-but-one syllable of a word: **Llanrhystud** – pronounce it 'thlan-rhu-stud' and you will be close!

KEY TO THE MAPS

– – – –	Walk route
✗ gate	Gate
S ✝	Stile
✗ SP	Sign post
FB	Foot bridge
WC	Toilets
♀ ♂	Woodland
⛪	Church

THE COUNTRYSIDE CODE

• Be safe – plan ahead and follow any signs

• Leave gates and property as you find them

• Protect plants and animals, and take your litter home

• Keep dogs under close control

• Consider other people

The CroW Act 2000, implemented throughout Wales in May 2005, introduced new legal rights of access for walkers to designated open country, predominantly mountain, moor, heath or down, plus all registered common land. This access can be subject to restrictions and closure for land management or safety reasons for up to 28 days a year. The following web site operated by Countryside Council for Wales will provide updated information on any closures.
www.ccw.gov.uk/countrysideaccesswales